The jump rope

Story by Jenny Giles

Illustrations by Sharyn Madder

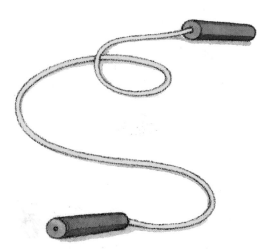

Abby always liked to play
with her friend Clare.
Clare lived on a farm.

"What can we do today?" said Abby.

"Let's jump rope!" said Clare.
"I can get two ropes from the shed."

"But I can't jump rope," said Abby.

"Make the rope go over your head, like this," said Clare. "Then jump!"

Abby tried, but she tripped.
She looked at Clare,
who was jumping very fast.

"I can't do that," said Abby.

"I had to try lots of times,"
said Clare,
"and then, one day, I did it."

Abby tried again and again,
but she still tripped over the rope.

Abby turned the rope one more time.
She let it stay on the ground,
and then she jumped over it.

"That's better!" said Clare.

"But I'm still not very good at it,"
said Abby. "I want to jump like you."

"The rope is too long for you,"
said Clare.
"I have a better one in my toy box.
Let's go and get it."

Abby looked at the rope.
"**That** is a good one!" she said.
"Thanks, Clare."

Abby ran outside with the rope.

She made it go over her head.

Then she jumped

as it came down to her feet.

And this time, she did **not** trip!

13

Abby turned the rope
around and around.
She jumped over it
without tripping at all.

"I can do it!" she shouted.

15

"Look, Clare!" laughed Abby.

"I can jump rope like you now!"